Exegesis of Despotism

Kuir ë Garang

The Nile Press
Calgary, Alberta

Copyright © 2012 by KUIR ë GARANG

All rights reserved. No part of this book may be reproduced or transmitted in any form or by any means, electronic, mechanical, photocopying or recording, without written permission of The Nile Press.

First Edition 2012
Second Edition 2015

ISBN: 978-0-9938279-3-8
PUBLISHED BY THE NILE PRESS
http://www.thenilepress.com
Calgary
Printed in USA

To my family with love
Mum (Ajah),
Kuirdit,
Nyibol,
Aguar,
Lual,
Awut,
Ador
and Atet

The very same new conditions that will on the average lead to the levelling and mediocritization of man—to a useful, industrious, handy, multi-purpose herd animal—are likely in the highest degree to give birth to exceptional human beings of the most dangerous and attractive quality.[1]

---

[1] Nietzsche, Friedrich. *Beyond Good and Evil.* New York: Vintage Books, 1966, p.176.

TABLE OF CONTENTS

PREFACE	**11**
SECTION ONE	**15**
Love, Life and Wonder	15
Poetic Preamble 1	17
Love the Apparition	20
Love Is Strange	23
Inconsequential Hearts	24
Death	25
In Time You'll Stand	27
Hypocrisy	28
The Admired	29
I Just Can't	30
The Other Lad's Girl	31
Flip Flop	32
The Love Game	33
Torturous Nights	34
Was It a Crack or a Gap?	35
Hope and Despair	36
The Come Back	37
Grandma's Cooking in a 'Calabash'	38
The Bath	40
Boarding School Prayers	41
Headmaster's Remark	42
The Verse and the Girl	43
The Perilous Path Dad Chose	44
SECTION TWO	**47**
Humanity and Misconceptions	47
Poetic Preamble 2	49
Why I Read	53
Will The Doors Open?	54
Great Expectations	56
Space and Time, the Little Girl	57

Hiding	59
Expectations I	60
Expectations II	61
Sister, Your Best You Is You	63
The Janitor	65
Individual Endeavours	66
The Hare and the Lion	67
Nature's Fave	68
Seasons, the Grass' Problem	69
Still Not Priggish	71
Pyrex Conundrum	73

SECTION THREE — 75

Nationhood, Suffering and Perceptions — 75

Poetic Preamble 3	77
The African Warrior	79
Cradle of Plight and Cradle of Joy	80
Aesthetic Drainage	81
Your Excellencies	82
The Tick Natters	83
Shattered Dreams Will Do the Impossible!	84
Profits of Death!	85
A skeleton with Grace	87
Fleeing Populace	88
Peace Now!	90
Southern Sounds	91
Diamond Seeded Mango's Cage	92
As I Die Slowly	93
Dragon Unleashed (1)	94
Dragon Unleashed (2)	95
Only a Jungle Beast, They Say.	96
Midday Dust Storm	97
To Disport Myself When the Pylon IS Cut	98
Exegesis of Despotism	99
Montreal Summer Sunset	100
The Avaricious Owl	101
The Nilotic Beam	102

Hope Candelabrum	103
Cinnamon Haunted	104

SECTION FOUR — 105

Religion, Nature, Being and Perceptions — 105

Poetic Preamble 4	107
What About Blackness?	110
Pious Rascals	111
The Cosmological Balls	112
I'll Wipe Them and Say Your Name Loud	113
Against Jejune Fidelity	115
A Ghostly Paragon	117
Spite Allayer I (Turning the Other Cheek)	119
The Chameleon Mercies	120
Feeler for Roses	121
The Bus Driver	122
Spite Allayer II (Altruism)	123
Even the Numb Nature Needs Joy	124
True Piety	125
What about Answers?	126
Word Document!	129
Scalpels of the Throng	130
Finding Cracks in Walls	131
Contentment I	133
Contentment II (Stygian)	134
The 'They' Conundrum	135
Rustic Ordeals	138
Synod Aspirations	139
The Winter	140
When Pigs Lend Hands	141
Your hair	142
Confidence	143

SECTION FIVE — 145

Appreciation — 145

Poetic Preamble 5	147

Just the Other Day	150
Festive City	151
The Strength of Your Whisper	152
When Nature is Questioned	153
Mum	154
Blessings of Bridge Builders	155

PREFACE

A person, who is born into a war condition, lives as a refugee for years, and then settles in a culturally diverse environment, is bound to have numerous experiences whose insightful evaluations are—most of the time—perplexing. These perplexing experiences can sometimes be vexing and at times humorous if given appropriate context.

Most of the poems in this collection were inspired by my experiences in warzones, my life as a refugee in different African countries, and more importantly, my life in Canada, a country whose cultural diversity has vast interpretive richness.

Obviously, living in a warzone raises many unsettling questions for inquisitive minds. Besides the fact that war reduces the affected populations to mere objects of play by the perpetrators of war, war also produces defiant spirits of reflection by destitute but blessed minds. However, the questions, which inquisitive minds ask, aren't answered to the satisfaction believable to those minds. One is confronted by unsympathetic loads of self-serving, self-righteous *pied pipers* intent on benefiting from shameless propagandizing in a manner that's detrimental to the 'objects of war.'

Besides this unfortunate realities of war, living in a culturally diverse environment is at times a blessing and at times an inquisitive minds' disturbance. However hard one tries to understand the medley of cultural contextualization of multiculturalism, one is still faced by numerous sceptical gazes peering deep into one's soul while drawing shallow conclusions about a judged self. There's always, with no doubt, a prevalent spirit of unease, discomfort and the implicit (at times required) element of damning 'otherness' in multicultural societies. Liberal idealism, however, covers up the ills of multiculturalism to make multiculturalism appear like the best panacea for inter-cultural, inter-ethnic and inter-racial understanding.

However, thinking minds will always find ways to put social contradictions into personal, fulfilling perspectives. This is meant (or it is supposed) to bring about a productive cultural phenomenon that's important to cohesive existence and understanding, if that is not at all naïve.

The collection of the poems in *Exegesis of Despotism* will follow the same poetic, thematic line presented in *Carcass Valley*. The poems celebrate the resilience of human spirit in the face of plight engendered by the destruction of war. The poems also celebrate the simple things in life such as jealousy, love, death, and birth. However, what the reader will find inherently salient in this poetry collection is the defiance towards the assumption different races make about themselves. And these tired generalizations are not, in this collection, limited to any race. All races make unflattering and unwarranted generalizations against other races. This state of affair is duly being mocked here along with its survivalist intent.

God, religion and metaphysical reflections on some of the things human beings deal with in their day-to-day lives are vocally presented. Poems such as *Pious Rascals* and *I'll Wipe Them and Say Your Name Loud* are two good examples of providential contradictions.

There'll be brief exegetical, *poetic preambles*, which the reader is advised to read critically before taking on the relevant sections. These *preambles* will help the reader appreciate the poems better.

With poetic hopes, I plan to take the reader on an emotional, intellectual and mundane *continental ride* through the mind of a war-child—a child who's been intellectually agitated, emotively metamorphosed, and culturally inspired.

Lastly—beside the effects of war—I cannot forget to appreciate the simple things I cherish: *country, family and the desire to learn*. I will then bring the reader back to her/his seat with a sigh that'd better be personally interpreted in order to make an epistemic sense.

Kuir ë Garang

Calgary, Alberta,

September 23, 2011

(revised November 14, 2015)

SECTION ONE

Love, Life and Wonder

Poetic Preamble 1

At one time or another, we've either been loved by someone, or we've loved someone. We've either hurt someone or we've been hurt by someone we loved. This is a cycle of love we all go through. A person who hasn't gone through this cycle might, one day, go through it. However, I'd still give some exceptions to people who might not go through this cycle either out of fortune or misfortune. That is perfectly acceptable and normal.

Besides the elements of love, this section will also give readers a sense of how others see us as persons, how our own work affects other people and how everyday experiences affect us and people we see around: at work, at school, in the cinema or any place where diversity is salient.

In *Love the Apparition,* there is a sense of wonder as to what love is and to what extent someone, who is in love, loses a sense of reality when completely love-struck. In *I Just Can't,* a person who is able to do a lot of things is so much affected by prejudgment around her so much so that her sense of direction becomes confused. And in *Torturous Nights*, we come to know how nights stagnate when those we love come to our minds. In *Death*, we get to see how important death is in our daily lives, especially its equalizing reality.

No matter what we do and who we are, love makes us wonder about some of the things that happen around us. We also wonder about the intricate manner in which nature designs the inexplicable complexities of human relationships, formal and informal.

While love is something we can't escape whether we are in a relationship or not, being loved is the most fulfilling phenomenon one will ever experience. This is something that is done to us without our effort. However, loving someone is unsettling, agitating and always unsatisfying. No matter what we think of people we love and whatever their feelings are towards us, loving them is a task we have to do. It is daunting and endless until (or unless) a conclusive end is arrived at.

And when too much thought is put into how a group of people is regarded (or judged), and how they interpret their image becomes dissatisfying, there is no amount of love you can give them to change them. Historically oppressed people are always categorized in a given socio-political niche. Most, if not all historically oppressed people, are born with the burden of history and their identity. Their values and characters are set before they even learn how to act. Essentially, this is a great human disservice this collection toys with.

Lastly, the reader wouldn't wonder too much as to why thoughts of death make everything—*social differentials*—disappear. Death makes us think of ourselves and nothing else: no fame, no riches, no high social status etc. Death is the most significant equality-engenderer and assurer. No one will ever say: 'Boo! You'll die but I won't!' Steve Jobs, in his June 12, 2005 commencement address to Stanford

University graduating students, rationalized death in this simple but nuanced philosophical precise:

> Remembering that I'll be dead soon is the most important tool I've ever encountered to help me make the big choices in life. Because almost everything — all external expectations, all pride, all fear of embarrassment or failure — these things just fall away in the face of death, leaving only what is truly important. Remembering that you are going to die is the best way I know to avoid the trap of thinking you have something to lose. You are already naked. There is no reason not to follow your heart.

Feel love and wonder about life!

Love the Apparition

For all the ones in love

Mrs. and Mr. Love, the anonymous!
You've always whistled, passed by and
I laughed, happy at the songs you both
Sang at Christmas as you put up
Neon lights and the Christmas tree.
I've always shelved my curious concerns.

You've always dressed in that velvet
Top barely reaching your belly, tight jeans
That I guess demanded your time and
Calories. Mr. Love always loved that.

You've always watched her bare belly
Button, infatuated by that pink ribbon
That always governed her wild hair.
Her boss at McDonalds always
Wondered about the feel of her hair.
What a schmuck!

Your neighbours have always cautioned
Me against the songs that eased
The *tough* out of my summer school.
I guess they were right...only for that
Stupid pink ribbon...and...and that
Velvet top.

The concerns I shelved behind the songs
Have gone bad as the cabinet onto which
I'd condemned them stinks with the

Mockery of your neighbours

Young Sarah laughed at me last night
As I unconsciously sang one of your
Wedding songs. She was sitting on her
Grandpa's house threshold. She always loved
That old, green *Ford truck* I drive to the farm.
But now young Sarah smiles, but shakes her
Head.

Mrs. Jones, with her white coffee cup, orange
Gum and brown teeth, told me young Sarah
Now sees Santa's belief written all over me.
I still believe in Santa I guess.
She's just ten, you know...

Mrs. love, I guess Shaggy was right.
You must be god, the care, your quiddity (loveliness)
Kept me going. But are you real? Do you even exist?
Perhaps anti-your-existence fellows are right?
Stupid me *believes* in Santa! Should I
Even doubt your existence?

Mr. love, I guess Carlin was right.
No women gods can create a universe
As unprincipled as this tired and miserable
One. You must be a man to create
Such a darn universe.

So, now, Mrs. and Mr. love, even
If I still believe in Santa, I've drunk
That colorless enlightenment liquid
Called scepticism. Now I say:

Love the apparition come...
The invisible, touchless force.

Love Is Strange

When they walk their hearts are set for fame,
But who knows if they can all be the same
In a world in which cultures clash by strength,
And survival is measured by length
To give the most dreaded the benefit of the weak…
That stirs sentiments in the underprivileged that survives no week,
….morning comes with feigned relief that disappears by night fall.

Inconsequential Hearts

They entered that white tent with a vivid Euphoria,
Dressed in that dreadful white like the Jewish
Messiah...We've escap*ed gloom into everlasting* H'ness.
Who should blame them...products of unlikely
'Indoctrinaire...'
They've praised and exalted themselves
As their opportunities whisked them higher than
They thought possible. They sent their pet to Alaska...it
Still remained their pet...but they thought better
Of what they've done...the cat is changed. Smiles!
The society watched as the tent's occupants
Became incensed and disconcerted.
They still uttered that mundane and
Inconsequentialists' "we don't care!"
The "we don't care" haunted them like
A spectre over their paradise.
They've always believed the ancient pronouncement,
And it is their right to deny the inconsequentialism
Emanating from their non-conscientious conscience...Papa
will give them a nostrum...
But the anxiety of the inconsequential
Heart remains...H'ness[2] is many light years away...Because
we're watching...and we're coming!!

---

[2] Happiness

Death

I *My funny friend*

You think you scare me...but I don't know you
You think you take lives away, perhaps it is not you
You think you're bad, perhaps life there is good
You think you have a name but you're only a misnomer
You think you are esteemed, but you're desperate...
Sure desperate for praise...then pride in lives gone
Death, my funny friend
You think you're cruel, but life six times beats you
I wait for you every single day...then you lie to me
You tell me scary stories of your game...just to be counted
Be glad cowards count you in their existential counts
Death my funny friend...
Death, you can't scare me
Death, you're a coward...
Death, you're lazy...
Death, do your own work…
Death, tell me how you actually operate,
Death, don't claim somebody's work,
Death, you're risking plagiarism...
Death, I boo you.
Death, my funny friend

II *My good friend*

The arrogant pride vainly but he's humbled by thoughts of you
Humanity is stratified but you humble all into a single equality
We could have claimed infinity of our existence but for you

We'd have been lazy in life's pursuit, but time is of essence
You've always scared us into thoughtfulness, should that be?
Rituals, protective creeds, greed and sacrifice all for fear of you!
Death, my good friend
I hated you but growth freed me to see the light of you
You aren't at all noxious… but an egalitarian campaigner
You, the only mirror of our confused cosmic populace
Time makes sense when you pass close by
Secrets reveal their hide-outs on smelling your scent
You squeeze kindness out of the hard-hearted when you strike
Death, you aren't malicious
Death, you give a choice of *the* end
Death, history has shown you're generous with time
Death, you make the stupid wise
Death, you make criminal loved
Death, you aren't arrogant
Death, you solace the abandoned
Death, you have the *same* face for many races
Death, you're the only *real* entity
Death, you're the only reality
Death, you aren't an illusion
Death, thanks for your egalitarianism
Death, you promise to come
And do so…
Death, my good friend!!

In Time You'll Stand

I don't know how to pray; I could've, for you, prayed.
I'm not souled else I could've, of substance, paid.
I'll hold yo' plight in heart until my time visits me grayed:
I'm by time reminded of yo' sorrow…nothing is left unsaid.

Disaster visited you impoverished, disdained and disowned…
Discover still yo' inner strength, the time you let go and grown.
Diseased by work, you stood; you cruised and laughed blown…
Disservice that dogged you was your superior's fear…stoned.

Gather your strength, and gather the energy of your laugh.
Grab your middle *passage resilience*…you know your tough
Glories, stories, and niches no one can assume when life's rough.

Souled voices had seen that mighty castle go down and hissed.
Their pockets were disturbed in an invariable actional process and eased
Some of your pain. Mind not the engineer and engineering: they were pleased.

Hypocrisy

A good child on the bridge
A smart child on the streets
A gifted child's tendency for kicks
A poor child's hope to ease
Her head into a comfortable squeeze
Of a warm pillow after she eats,
A rich child's hope to help peace
Dawn on every poor soul…
All are just prayers as the societal
Hypocrisy preys on the poor.

The Admired

The heavy weight you carry
Speaks out your inner strength,
You perform it as if you're in a hurry
To stretch out your arm a length.
That's the glamour desired.

They just stand bewildered and stare
At your risky, artistic balancing
Of the giant weight...they "care"
About that precarious dancing.
They've wondered, you, the admired.

Their concern increases to bear.
To bear as you're accosted, solacing.
But they're scared at your facial flare.
You stare contemptuously, menacing.
But know you...you're the admired.

I Just Can't

I have a pen
But can't write,
I have a book
But I can't read,
I have a teacher
But I can't listen,
A pen,
A book,
And a teacher,
What are they to me?
I'm sick
But I can't die,
I'm hungry
But I can't eat,
I'm sad
But can't cry,
Sickness,
Hunger,
And sadness,
What will you do me?
I'm big
But I'm treated small,
I have a head
But I'm applied as a hand,
I pop up
But I'm hit back in,
My bigness,
My head,
My emergence,
Will you make me?!

The Other Lad's Girl

Far in front, wasp-waisted and groomed,
She clasped her papers on her chest, then loomed

The elitists' sprouting of floweret burgeoning.
As she stole a supersonic peek at me, she stood beckoning.

I then felt heated, eyes beamed at me, from scalp to the toes.
Bathed in sweat, fear; emotion emptied my skull. She knows?

Flip Flop

When I consult my thoughts and think
Of you as I look into my dirty sink,
The figure *he* gives me looks the same,
But the game *he* plays suggests some name
That pushes *us* seemingly to the rear,

A thing that I thought would not bear
Any truth, but there *he* is with mocking looks
With our girl, that tells me nothing in books,
But only to suggest that you need to change,
As you sway your beams, a duck in the range,

I guess, with naivety, the trust is never betrayed,
Even if doubt is irresponsibly portrayed,

But the party that was supposed to serve
And lead by example, when others have not a nerve,
Now, treads, tramples on your assumed range,

The cast of doubt leads the good to the thinking,
That all they had in store is going down sinking,
With nothing they can do to have the course change,
But the reciprocation misleads the good in exchange
Of self-protecting word aimed at relieving the pain,
But when the truth downs, you flicker, slicker flip flop.

The Love Game

They took the vivid green game
To see if they could get the name,
But the clarity was not the same, When the psychic
deviations assumed the main
Know-how of what made them lame,

But they all slumbered when they came
To the realizable dogma of the game,
That gave 'em hope they thought would tame
Him, but they curved home the jealous hand
Realizing they didn't know the man.

Torturous Nights

It was quiet and pitch black that night,
My heart whispered just about right,
But calm married to loneliness sides
With the unbroken misery to exalt waves
Of destructive emotional execution,

Through the loss that still bites
Through, across the crack every night,
Gathering my naivety and loss like tides
Poised to destroy humanity by waves,
You had me bleeding, a leftover potion.

But as every night visits with light
Comfort gone, and holding-you-tight
Memories become epical as the guides
That have turned the motherly night ways,
The comfort, as soothing as its passion,

Into torturous 12 to make them feel 8736…

Was It a Crack or a Gap?

The wind piteously
Licked my tears
As it climbed crowds
Of heavenly
But cannot-be-seen stairs,
Leaving me with stares
Of a bewildered brother
With ten-years-job iced.
I knew it was too white,
Cold snowy day, yet my heart
Blackened it with thoughts of you,
'Black despair' like my own skin.
I didn't accept you'd gone.

So gone you sigh,
Far up there so high,
Like a cat's rejection
Of water I stuck to you—no passion.
Like a tick to a cow—poor action.
But my mouth held too
Weak a grip, too soon
My heart was axed,
Excruciating gap
Rimmed not a crack
But a huge, emotional gap.

Hope and Despair

By the fire place
It is all quiet, cold
And mocking; yet it seems
To whisper to me, that
You'll ring a come-back,

To inject life into me
Just by the sight of you,
Punctuated by that crispy
And soulful voice
To just 'I love you' me,

It sounds so naïve, feels
Like nothing, yet so dauntingly
Heavy as I weigh you in my head,
The phone in hand like a lottery
Hopeful, thinking you will call.

Meekly, I stare at the laughing
Flames that's mocking me, but I know,
Far from the empty craving,
Something in you and me *shall* shine.

The Come Back

I didn't have to look twice;
I might have been wrong,
But my conscience was bathed
In everything *you* as I gasped
To reach, breathe and crave
The sight of you, the feel of you.

Yet the soul that is the man
I am, stiffed with both fear and archaic
Amazement like the uncertainty
Of the first time hunter,
And (the truth) my head air-tight,
Emptied by nothing but you.

And as you brushed me off with ease,
Just like a fly by the elephant's eyes,
I still waited.

So when the truth settled upon you in
The dead of night, perhaps in
Broad daylight, reminded by our
Ancestral innocence…
Your eyes hooked open and wide,
You sprinted back to the spot you then belittled,
Only to find out that it was not
My turn to wait.
You fell in, fried in your come back.

Grandma's Cooking in a 'Calabash'

Submerged in that sea
Of dangerous cattle heads,
I thought of no life
Beyond the cows'
Significance, but I fixed my head
In the glory of my ancestral
Story with a distilled water heart, head:
No jealousy, no hate, no worries,
Because all that mattered to me
Was the varied coloration
Mooing around me, serving me the
Solace unequalled anywhere,
With scared legs and bruised
Hands, still, I stood admiringly, marvelling
At how these creatures got me, yet couldn't tell me
The beauty in them.
I thought I'd be there for ever,
But someone told me
Grandma needed me home *now*.

They summoned me home,
Oblivious of what they wanted done,
And Like a thirsty *thiang,* I came running
Home to grandma's cooking,
Food that eats you the much
You eat it to your fill…
Twenty mouthfuls you'd think, far from the
Occidental, maybe next to the oriental,
But all didn't matter because the hyena's mouth
The food gives you, yeah! Did I tell you

Why they called me? You'd never guess!
Grandma's cooking is so jealous,
Never let you talk something else,
Everything is forgotten—enforced, maybe!
As I eagled down on the calabash
With *tung* and *thial* angled with coveted
Precision, I thought not, I just ate hot!

Waking up from grandma's
Cooking-eating reverie, I saw Ajak,
Adorned in green-yellow-black
Khaki, like a rock-faced soldier
Marshalling to a firing squad,
Swung his gun in style and elegance,
Looking on I thought he looked like
A paramount chief, primed and adorned for a
Godly gala; and I stared blithely
At his small contraption, which he said
Could make me sleep forever if angered,
But yet, in all that oblivion, they told me:
Your mum is in Baidit, we're going,
Oh no, it wasn't even eleven, it was five mouthfuls
That engrossed, so sad! My grandma's cooking was left,
Till five years later! How sad?

The Bath

Wizened but she thought it was for *a* minx,
Slender, curved, and …
The enchantress was razzed
By the excessiveness of the ratio,
Which she thought the bath
Could engender!

Strolled, flirtatious with confidence,
Which guided her feigned satisfaction,
Transient, she didn't know,
The outward hip never
Woos for nature is not crass,
And that bath is but a tort.

She thought she'd left
All the 'wooed' smutty,
Which the cosmic demands ever made.
She saw them: *the plebeians*,
Lowered in her choice by nature,
But the bath, she'd come to understand,
Was no panacea, the smutty she'd left
 Still had a room when she 'turned!'

Boarding School Prayers

He was defiantly upright on the
Dining hall podium,
His voice thunderously
Threatening, voicing his message
With prefects perfectly policing
Before he blessed something
That looked like food with
A microsecond prayer,
Not a second lest no one prayed:
Would be too long a prayer,
For heat's and hunger's punches
Only receded three months
Away from then.
Meanwhile, what there was,
In those trays,
Was swallowed in peace and minds
    Bound to it,
Three months *there* was three decades.

Headmaster's Remark

Papally mannered, nobly
Dressed, he electrified the air
With wise sayings, but who was
Heeding him? 'Pretending' they
Said of him.

They didn't need being
Suffused with scholarly
Smartness,
'It's more freedom and more food
We want…you're talking to the buildings,'
They looked like saying.

Then the sun peeped behind his office
And the time keeper beat the bell
To yell, then again, the sun stretched
Her neck further: 'Is he still wising them?'
She seemed to be saying.

Then teachers started to squirm in discomfort:
'He's *breaking* English again… it is
Not a sermon… election is far away,'
Their eyes seemed to say.

'With those few remarks I'll end there,
I don't want to bore you, wise people are not
Given many words,'
'But sir, an hour of words is not a remark,
But a sermon,' the dispersing students seemed to say.

The Verse and the Girl

Denial mothers the meanest of cruelty, but it still
Serves and saves when times calls, I write and will,
Wheel away, having jotted a verse about Mary,
The title paradoxical yet amusing the girl I'll marry.

Symbolic was the last line, emotion serving, crude
Like an unexpected neoteric theorem, that a rude
Mathematician has unearthed giving him emblems, marks,
The disavowed accolade placing everyone else on the racks.

In the morning she called, 'who could that be?'
I lonely hushed, hands shaking writing the word 'thee'
It was 'we' I wanted rhymed, 'what's that noise I hear?'
She said, 'writing again?' No, I denied, she's my ear.

The Perilous Path Dad Chose

We left and crossed the river over the
Deafening sounds of rumbling
Anger of raging arsenals,
Dad wanted us safe, crossing
The Nile was our only hope,
We'd crossed the river, but ubiquitous
The brick anger was, we'd reached
Talle by midday: serene, desolate and intact the
Town was, the residents had fled
For safety, but there we trod
In front of angry lions with
Teeth and hearts set for
Flesh and innocent preys,
But behold! nature spoke,
Because dad was never wrong
And nothing he'd said slipped:
We'd sit by the road side when done for,
At times we'd trample the bushes' thickness
To reach the bushes' depths, to shadow us,
Giving us her seconds-to-minutes' heaven
As we kept clear of predators' paths:
Humans' and animals'…
Then we'd head back onto
The lonely roads…
Hop when strong,
Hope when tired,
Stop when safe,
And sing if prone to cries.
We made it to *Mundri* and *Kaya* weeks later,
Iron-hearted, dad would pick his *jembe* in rage,
Like the same heart that placed us

On the run, he'd be there in the fields
From dawn to midday,
'He who loves me will say continue, the
Hater says stop, it's too hot,' he'd tell me,
I'd seen his hand, *Garangdit*: gripping the
Jembe, weeding the cucumber, okra,
Yams, cassava, onions, potatoes.
I have nothing to sing, nothing to say, nothing
To live for, but his hand…
He made the world in us,
Dashed the peril of the lions, and the
Naivety of the enemy
In the end, his heart's grits
Afforded me the arctic realms.

SECTION TWO

Humanity and Misconceptions

Poetic Preamble 2

It's no secret that slavery and colonialism have left an unfortunate legacy that'll take centuries to dispel if dispelling it is at all possible, or required. 'Third World' countries sometimes argue that they—except Europe and countries with predominantly European populations—and more so, Africa, are the way they are because of disenfranchisement and dependencies caused by colonialism and slavery. This view-point is rationalized as weakness-inspired excuse by Africans and their 'Co-Third-worlders'. Africans, it is argued, tend to downplay their own soft spots and rush to blame Europeans and Americans for Africa's problems. There's some truth in that criticism because African corruption, while it's fuelled by 'western' capitalists, is unconscionably African.

However, the effects of *colonialism* and *slavery* have to be properly contextualized before being dismissed. Slavery and colonialism, undoubtedly, have left a mindset that will be difficult if not impossible to do away with.

In *Sister the Best You is You*, we see that African girls tend to look for some measure of beauty outside them, taking *that* outside rationalization of themselves as the only way for them to measure up to the standardized measure of beauty, in other words, Euro-centric concept of beauty. In *Hare and the Lion*, we get to debate the question of whether Europe or Africans are to blame for the mess in Africa. And in *The Janitor*, we understand that it is not only the rich and the educated, who are enlightened. Wisdom, appreciable and productive knowledge can be found in a *mere Janitor*. In *Expectation I*, we understand that, at times, we look down on Africans until (or unless) they do exactly what we never thought they could do. We don't think of Africans as capable of doing some things. We judge them before we even give them an opportunity to try in order for us to render our fair judgements.

It is important to add this on my part as a South Sudanese. *African Sudanese* have been looked down upon by the *Arabs Sudanese* because of all the misconceptions stemming from slavery and colonialism. It didn't matter how resourceful and educated South Sudanese became, they were still *'abeed'* (slaves) who shouldn't be allowed to *rule* or practice their social or religious practices. *Will the Doors Open* will help us understand that African plight.

The best way for us to do away with such misconceptions is to avoid things that reinforce the same misconceptions. One can only blame others if all the possibilities of one being blamed are done away with. Africans therefore should clean all their acts; corruption, leadership incompetence, tribalism, nepotism etc. There and then can they come and blame the *west* for historical misdeeds.

We however shouldn't be naïve as to quickly absolve Europe and the Americas of the historical and present misdeeds. Or even acknowledge all the historical misdeeds with sarcasm and modest condescension: "I acknowledge those mistakes even if I wasn't there. I'm sorry, but hey *Jack*; let's move on, can we?"

Issues such as favourable economic relations, selective levying of heavy tariffs on poor country's exports, economic protectionism, should be examined with care.

Let's think critically about our own humanity and how we perceive others so as to evaluate the authenticity of our judgments about others.

Why I Read

This stack of books excites me,
You wonder what whiff I see,
It might be an iota cognoscible,
But fear no advent of a *pied piper*.

I think...and pen...

Your affect in front, your zeal sees.
They count the expectation to be,
Huey Newton came recognizable,
Dilettantes feared the true cipher.

I listen...and craft...

Will The Doors Open?

Yes, it's time for referendum

They've always put the words in our mouths,
And we've always said the words to their desires.

They've also written our narrative upside down,
And we've paid them lump-sum gratitude.

You wonder why a diseased people in a far
Land want to tarnish the symbol of our livelihood!

The Nile is so far away...and the diseased doesn't
Know the Nile's beauty but she blames the Nile!!

No wonder others use my name to be humbled,
And they use my place to be richer and powerful.

The Nile blamers have always written my narratives
In their liking, demanding my respect for *the* work.

You've always shared in their denigration of the Nileans,
Well, a good number claim the name out of ignorance.

But I'm not whining I'm just writing my narrative
At the last hour...yes, I've seen the papers written.

I've also seen the boxes coming my way...just.
My old friend, I've increased the white substance

Inside my head and I'll soon be creating a
New house next to your, a house with a beautiful

Garden, a house surrounded by *neem* and *teek*.
I know you've always wanted me down.

Oh, I'm sorry, the black boxes have arrived and
Mohammed told me you'd always wanted to hide

A good number. No. We are watching at a distance
Because the doors have opened.

Great Expectations

The myriad of colors that enamoured you
Told a different narrative, a childish belief in Santa.
Life looked so bright when you were outside,
Looking down into the depth of the dam below.

The flow of the water reminded you
of the flow of your blood when you
Saw that glamour, class and promise
written all over that white suit.

You'd claimed, 'mummy, I've chosen.'
Honesty and affection came driving on
Four wheels, fast and furious and no
One blamed you then…just in the moment.

But you'd miscalculated the journey,
The driver had miscalculated the
The mileage, and reason for the journey
Had miscalculated his powers.

The mountain range behind you laughed
As you watched the car thin into the greenness
Of the hills behind, the reason scratching his head
And the driver with his head
Between his legs, saying: "He's just a kid."

Space and Time, the Little Girl

She was wire thin, really dark and short when I looked at
Her. Her left hand was pulled down by a dark-green bowl
Full of dirty Stuff and my assumed undesirables.
I looked Away feigning a distraction by a passing, rickety,
green Military truck.
When I Looked back again, she'd melted into a dingy,
dusty alley...

A week later she was rigidly standing in the same muddy
Spot Holding the same tired stuff as I stared at her,
Bewildered, Stupefied and ashamed.
Her left shoulder was always lower than her right shoulder.
Her piercing eyes reduced me to an itsy bitsy, but she held
her hand out and said:
"I make you uneasy, don't I?"

Friday afternoon as the sun stretched her orange tongue to
Bless The western reddening horizon with a kiss, the girl
Stood looking at me at a bus stop holding nothing but god's
Mercies and asked: "What's time and space?" 'I...I...I...' I
Was struck, lightning Struck by nothing but assumption.

"Time and space separates you and me, time and space
Separates what I own and what you own, time and space is
The reason you're tall and I'm short, time and space is the
Reason you're forty and I ten, time and space is the reason
You're a man and I'm a girl, time and space is the reason
You're not my husband, time and space is the reason I'm
Poor and you relatively ok, time and space is the reason
You're not our president...think time and space and
Anything...anything *IS...*"

Time and space perhaps brought me to the hospital a day Later....change in time and space does more...who're you little Girl...just time and space...?

Hiding

They've always hidden their *them*
Behind that heart-shaped red curtain.
Now the incontinent inevitable
Will fan its chill over the thought
Impossible. They say life starts with
A 'B' but they guess it starts with'
Should we be as open and as comfort-
Engendering as our breezy, open, blue seas?'
The mark, its christening and baptismal
Anointment will be their desired lesson.
Their words are sharp: they're
Keys, they're strength, and they're the light.
Let them use our words; let them sing
About the mystified phenomenon
Behind which they've built a life.
Let them not stop hiding: one way
Or another, they'll be fished out.

Expectations I

John squirmed as I got to the podium,
Jane giggled as I took the mic...
But then the lady on the stage waved
And all were grave-yard silent.
Then the ghosts in me struck and I saw
Jane's frown flattening, the terraces on
Her forehead slowly eroding.
"Get 'em the expected stigma...and the
Jaw-dropping serenade," my *me* said.
As my me-centredness ran wild, I saw John
Sitting up, high enough as he smoked my words;
Jane out-worldly silent as her *self* deserted her.
Relax...you didn't listen to me before you
asked...just stop!

Expectations II

She'd advised cordially and quietly when she told me I wasn't singing.
I couldn't fault her for she was seasoned: she'd said all she heard was a dirge;
But she was, in honesty, right; for all the world knows…a *fall guy* I am.

I've been menially helpful, supportive so she said I was too obeisant,
For anytime she removed that pink ribbon on her head, she Saw hypocrisy.
But she was right, 'cause all the time I wore a black ribbon, ok, a cypher I was!

With that black ribbon getting soaked with sweat, I talked too much.
All she saw was smiles with me, pretentious smiles to swear away the pain;
But she was right, the visible and invisible yokes were hard… miserable I should be!

Magical hands and muscles are marvelled about, but I was A disgrace to the living.
For all she saw was a weird sheep, a weird sheep she couldn't define so she described me: *Black!*
But she was right, however far I traveled, hard I worked; My place was just *colorfully* defined!

She saw the load and shook her head…saying the task would be hard for me.
Politicking and narratives hadn't prepared her.

The head and skin I was…
The head and the skin I carried were estranging.
Oh, the 'olds' dug the same.

Sister, Your Best You Is You

Don't look at that crimson dress
Because you'll always change it,
Don't frown at the mirror,
He's just being the only honest friend.
 How many friends tell you you for you?
 Sister, the best you *is* you!

Take that pen and write your name,
Don't tell me you don't know how!
Climb those stairs every day;
I hear talks of those miserable pounds.
The Hindland brother delights in
Bumps and curves...out of caves.
Sister, the best you they want *is* you!
Read that book and laugh silly and loud,
 Because the world loves you...
He lies when he says no... he dreams
Sweetly when he earns your glance,
Again, read that book and say...
I'm not a queen but I'm the Hindland
Face and mind: dark-faced, smooth-bodied...
What?...silly them, because
Your best you *is* you.

 Don't dream for gleams and glances,
 For all you lack is a platform;
Don't drink too much, because they
Need the word of the Hindland tongue;
Don't run after every drum, because
They'll always miss your mysterious input,
Damn them...silly them will always think:

The queen...no...the Hindland face
Will come, because, her best her is *she*!

Don't display your you, sister,
Because your you comes every never...
You'd breathed peace and calm when
The rest knew your *socratic* 'unmatchness,'
Why did they go prostrate before you... ?
Because the Hindland face had a platform.
Don't hate them, sister, they knew not
Their hearts...I mean the hearts with mammoth envy...

Again, don't display your you, display your
Soft white/grey matter inside your white hard matter.
Don't be seen sister, be a word in our every
Mouth, because your best you *is* you!

No, needn't I forget...Who'll read to me if you hate books,
Who'll explain the lies in *the book* if you hate books?
Who'll advise your female seeds to keep their chins up?
Sister, I miss... I see Hindland face But not the *Hindland mind*!

Because, the best you *is* you!

The Janitor

He hasn't seen the hibiscus growth,
But he still knows the hiccup's
Root and Route,

He hasn't seen where hibiscus grows,
But he values and reads the meniscus
The wisest he should,

His palms' toiling is the litmus
Of crystal living, ready to discuss
Typhoon and typhus—we also could.

Individual Endeavours

I walk a little, that is, by the roadside.
Then I stop and gaze. I have walked for
A long, long time and I have to rest, but they
Say I'm just young, maybe I imagine much.
The taste of life, crispy they say, is nothing
But bitterness that puts me onto the rack.
Is it my tongue? Maybe my heritage!

Then I walk on; cracking like 'ancient'
Automobile remains of colonial road glory;
My in-body feeling salty, peppery;
Bones cramping like boots on dry snow.
Everything, everyone smells of …

I walk on as the world around
Me revolves: meek, joyous, tired...
More than a million of mine, then
I fasten my paces.

Not that the gods had touched me.

We all live like life lists only a few
Into its Africa's book, perhaps heritage books,
 I toss my cynicism; I'm not alone.

The Hare and the Lion

On one clear African night, with a broom
In my hand, having heeded dad's quality,
With my siblings we sat around our animist feats.
Dad told us a story: he started of a cool fool.

'Once upon a time,' he said, 'in the the jungles
Of *Pan ë Jëïëng* and *Ngun Nuerë*[3],'

The lion humbly gave the hare his only room,
But with schemes the hare crossed hospitality,
And claimed himself the victor, with skids
He dominated and took the lion for a fool.

Lion's humility brought him the doom;
The hare's schemes withered in totality
The good natured valour of the lion's grits.
It ate internally lion's strength to an empty pool.

Lion's reality grasp pushed out the gloom
As the Hare's empathy upsurged: wished finality.
But the Hare's thought-arrogance had lion's seats…
The lion, battled to naught, opted to cool.

But the lion's will still filled the rill to boom,
And pregnant with ideas, the lion braved the reality
Of the Hare's thesis out of truth, not that it fits;
Leaving with lion's endowment, *lion's* now the least!

---

[3] *Pan ë Jiëng* and *Ngun Nuerë Jieng* (Dinka) and Nuer countryside, respectively

Nature's Fave

I'm here but I know you mum.
You graced my steps so I strut,
And the cat inside me presses
Me to swagger—can I buckle?
You sowed the cat in me and
Nature stamped it and I pose;
Not stooping to limit the grace
You hammered in me to nurture.
Though they press me to keep
Down; bad, dangerous I am, they think.
They press me to quietude but
The cat you planted in me presses
Me to simper but with known guts.
And surprised to their ridiculed belying,
They stand amazed at this nut.
Thanks: you blessed me mum,
And the cat that says no, no and no!
You should be there!

Seasons, the Grass' Problem

Green and they call you grass
Brown and they call you grass
Red and they still call you grass
Yellow and it looks like you don't change, grass
Birds inhabit you yet you're still the grass,
Jealousy or naivety of your cousins, trees,
Remember?
I may be wrong, sorry, perhaps chanced, please,
I think it's your home, dressed
By the beauty of nature, impressed,
But do all the names act as you're pressed?
That's the beauty that's fixed nowhere
Yet you still dazzle and brighten e'where?
You still ridicule your beauty dear grass,
Is it that they burn and misuse you, grass?
Where's your might, desist, will they exist?
Or is it that you don't know who you are?
Take the best though innumerable the definitions are,
When did they strike to plant fear in you?
Are they not dependent on you, aren't they?
You think technology's will
Helps them take you rear, but still
…but you give and receive at will,
Don't tell me that it was a steal.
Is it that you don't look the same?
Or is it because you change with season?
Or is it that your change is not a reason?
That they don't appreciate the level on
Which you are?
I think you have all to exist,

And all names will glorify all
The colors nature bestowed all over you,
You want to be weak, think what they think of you!
And technology will not mark you down,
They fear you, though weak you are,
You purify their air, yet you're disgusting?
Believe and seasonal names will exit.

Still Not Priggish

As the world basks
In the glittering tasks
With no whims of asking
Into its conscious gleams
Of humanity feel glimpse,
First, I ask myself naively:
Did I exist or do I exist?

But the mix of
White sepulchre,
And my drunkenness
Upon the abundance of history
Brews leaves
Ampleness of feeling
That prickles my zest,

And my…

Confused existences,
Identities!
And *searchings* of
My heart rightful
Position! Swallowed
And swallowed by that dreadful
Ocean and held by those nooses and
Unforgiving steels.

I wonder why narratives
Follow me? Still rocked in
Cubicles and locked out, a
Dunderhead,

Feared infectious
And dangerous
By both might and stupidity.
I don't know what to feel.
My blood ubiquitous
And historically 'zebrad'.

Pyrex Conundrum

Not *a* Pyrex, not even a real, begrudging weakling,
Not even a dodo, but, still in niggling
Mess, he hoists confidently his life's pylon
To Mars, because Jupiter's big, feared like a cyclone
And long way out of his ancestral reach.

Life gently runs by like summer sea waves,
And a glass water tabled and serenely housed,
But he still sees life as a pawky mistake, soused
For counts, but still sees purplish passage, caves
Of goodness perhaps; therein lies his ditch.

Because nothing he writes is violent enough,
His writings treats of grits but not so tough.
It's a ritzy might coughed into a dirty nylon.
The will is, with a purple passage, out and silent.

SECTION THREE

Nationhood, Suffering and Perceptions

Poetic Preamble 3

This section contains words about war and its aftermath. Most of the people adversely affected by war are the most vulnerable: children, women and the elderly. The destitution in which these victims are left in becomes unspeakably monstrously if no conscientious leaders come to their rescue through sound systems of government or humanitarianism.

Sudan and South Sudan have been mired in a state of war for more than *fifty years*. And the triggers of war, one has to remember, are due to misconceptions, and misguided feelings of superiority. These misconceptions are garnered from misunderstood interpretation of religious and cultural sentiments. In this section, I've tried to voice some of these misconceptions including the suffering endured not only by the Sudanese and South Sudanese people, but also by everyone whose life has been affected by the monstrosity of war.

There's also *the* haunting spectre of how Africans and people of African descent are perceived and treated by the rest of the world. Sometimes these crass perceptions of Africans are covered-up with wicked paternalism, patronage and condescension. In a sense, these perceptions are at times unconscious and at times voluntarily effected. Fanon would call this state of affair the 'collective unconscious' of the oppressive *other*. In addition, it's true to say that these perceptions are derived from Africa's historical derivatives, economic backwardness or stagnation, constant being in a state of war and the inability of Africans to deal with epidemics such as HIV/AIDS, and abject poverty. This situation is underscored by the deplorable nature of Africa's leadership and governance.

Exegesis of Despotism helps us understand how African leaders exploit the average citizen with the help of foreign non-conscientious super-capitalists, and immoral investors. This disenfranchisement is executed with the help of African leaders, who wield iron fists against the very ones they should be protecting: citizens.

> ....but fortune
> Of the destitute naps too long for enough, and fortune
> Of the despot stays bright and shine, for it eats big and plant ample petard
> That the weak squirm with their words only squeezed out in fright, hard
> And desired, and the master joyous, drifting, sailing high in ecstasy
> Far beyond the leaps and hop of his iron hands, 'cause his
> Scratchy Demeanour's bitter, ...

Aesthetic Drainage helps us understand the manner in which brain-drain is affecting Africa through foreign enticements. *Profits of Death* explains how selfish, non-conscientious super-capitalists benefit from situations such as 'Blood Diamond' and 'Blood Oil.' This breed of capitalists gets a lot of assistance from African leaders in order to execute their unfettered exploitative practices.

The reader will have to read with an open mind.

Open your mind and explore Africa with intellectually informed sensibility!

The African Warrior

(For them who died)

Why was it the strength
Of the warrior's will that made
Them wild and condensed
The warrior?

Vaporized for coveted paternity:
Iron of all irons,
By will and word,
Diamond of all grits.

He stood and took
From valour, descended
With a few alien drops,
He pretended not, blinked not.

He had a job. He talked.
He defied, he prided, he
Grew from true branches
Of a deep rooted plant.

His chord was nature
Shaped for *it*; night, day,
He did it, and taken by
It: the word he believed.
Who can take it on?
Now they want his ghost
Tainted, because his spirit and
Courage, live on.

Cradle of Plight and Cradle of Joy

Bright years away, I wish
The lionesses knew.
The rest picked up
Their smooth, finely embroidered
Regal linen…
Just ceremoniously.

But the lionesses piece their pieces to
Scale away heat, rain prickles… all nature's
Bites, that is, if the pieces neatly
Overlap like the scales of fish.

The lionesses' trials are all patched up in love;
The mammoth tasks geared all for survival.

Aesthetic Drainage

The drainage of knowledge
He didn't know, has no
Colored reminder, because
That mighty apparition
Hops from body to body;
Too powerful, a cannot-be-seen
Destroyer, at times a sober
Savior—he's neither, just absorbed!
When the *giver* seats the
Given, a token for the job *well-done,*
The given's ecstasy erases not alone
The epitome of the *given's* own.
That epitome lights the path of
The *given,* to see the *giver* in that even
Western sophistication-uneven.
He sits there with a sober well-being.

Your Excellencies

Boss, the master knew his takes,
Canonized he might have
Looked, but smart thieves, chiefs.
You'd pushed the master away,
With his belongings gathered with
A resentful gaze by the door, he's not really
Gone, has he? He eats you in methods!
Don't ask me with a frown.
Boss, now you messed it, like
Some uncertain ingrate, you're all
The same: he set you up, now you
Drain me, do I pity you, me?
No, now the master laughs at you;
Dressed regally and sighs: *we told them*
History is a preferred narrative.
Boss, he left you; hoping
You'd fair miserably, and miserable
You have done.
The master race (d) (s) you down,
Then laugh (s) (ed), 'ha! ha! didn't I say
That that man couldn't,' he muses.

The Tick Natters

Dressed in priestly calico, he imagines
Ducal, princely airs of totality; shamelessly
Owning, but they're all steals.
With shameless
Deprivation he matches to lies processing:
A dunce, a dunderhead, but he looks suited
Up like a learned noble man.

His walking, call it, stealing to kneeling stick,
Thrushed up into the air; a show of *kingship*
Maintained with a *hard* fist.

He drains collections of the same innocent
Souls that still scream praises, oblivious of
How the monster demands their blood;
Canoodling them eloquently,

"The honourable, they say, we love you!"

Shattered Dreams Will Do the Impossible!

I didn't see vapid grasps of dint,
Acrid, stagnant ideological miscarriages
That were thought preceded the claims
When the claimant's dreams and hopes
Fell and scattered, shattered; throwing multi-colored
Butterflies of wasted dreams like human flesh
Blown to pieces by the unmerciful
Russian planes, and like feces of a madman
Held up as weapons.
With this though, he's still
Fixed and mocked, enjoyed,
Mockers' feelings hidden,
Truest intent smoking dreams
Away in a pipe whose inner shape
Mirrors their seen and thought "being."
They may not be believers in any known
Mockery, but the shattered dreams
Will be collected. Impossible?

Profits of Death!

Where birds hold and sharpen
Their spears
In readiness of the boom to happen
Who fears?
Who're they?
Who dare speak for them, pray?

Capitalists empty their banks
Expecting pence in sounds of tanks,
Worthless, profitable creatures!
Have long to go to get their treasures?
Bankers triumphed, will they?
Bankers schemed, moralists say.

Praised by birds descending like flies,
Their madness feeds the skies,
On this earth: *a mere inhabitant*.
The capitalists have come a distant.
Bankers, capitalists and earth's avian
Visitors now blame the Asian,
Worthlessness and usefulness today!

Every death of *one* is a 10^6 dollars defined
To the one who says *worthless creatures!*
Yet birds in their ways know their statures.
They thank god not for the dollars mined.
It's their flesh all the way!
Abundant meal everyday!

That is where *worthless creatures* belong!
They gave the *creatures* the knife to be 'strong;'

The sword and schooled them for a praise song.
The Banker, the Explorer, and the Capitalist run
Not that they've been scotched by the sun,
They'd dug up the mighty D out of that clay
Nassau, Kingston, Cancun call *who* after the pay?

A skeleton with Grace

Only ten but she looks sixty.
She doesn't worry about it though,

For all that rumbles in her
Bulging head and diminishing body,

Is how to fill that brown mug
With three grains of maize,

That she woefully awaits
Like a chick who looks up expecting

Mom's hunt, yet, that mom descends,
Pregnant with food and humans,

Doesn't serve her, because *whatever*
Grain that falls, serves only the *muscled*.

Fleeing Populace

I see a sea of screaming children,
Silent sweating mothers;
With mothers battered, beaten in turn
By the weight of their enormous loads;
The human file sandwiched between trees rows,
The loads press them down, crippling them
With each step of the journey, every time;
Night or day, they tread on those pregnancies:
Swampy waters conceive of
Snakes, scorpions, spiders, centipedes…
And all the venomous creatures!

The string of the fleeing file of humanity builds
An unbroken stream of wasted flesh,
The sight of all defy a push of one's optical
Perspective; the perspective is dwarfed
By the endless file, infinite mass that seems to go
Somewhere, yet nowhere, comes from somewhere yet
Nowhere! Static, yet moving!

The birds then gather to celebrate wasted mass
Of humanity that falls short of hope and
Materials to reach their craved, prayed-for "haven,"
Marching bodies glance at the feasting avian
Material, but dare not grip any defiant look,
Lest they be feasted on: because they look nothing
But *walking-dead*.

Thirst demands a sizeable part of the already diminishing
Populace that guns keep resizing, pangs of hunger prick

Into the heart of the file and it looks static, yet moving!
I ask: how many reach there!?

Peace Now!

She wouldn't lay any more low,
Because we've all seen and we'll know,
That she'll stay upright for what she sow,
And what providence served her though,
Was cooked to weigh her as a spurn.
But now she says: "Yeah, toss me high!"

We still holds on to our clear cut caprice,
But she'll hold no premonition, are we surprised?
We shouldn't be because the thought was nice,
For she'd let us think foolish and fantasize;
That her mind's state was a nightmarish incertitude,
But now she says: "Yeah, toss me high!"

Nature perorates no dogmatic mindset,
But nature serves her with *that* from sunset,
She held it then, now so high, don't think of reject,
Because she has a heart that for it we'll reset,
Let's learn now for time won't be bet,
Because all she says now is: "You'll toss me high!"

Southern Sounds

The lorry's engine rattles; the lorry twists as if in pain
As it cries its way up the hill before the rain,
With a *clattering* under is a shrieking mechanical connection,
The driver, bathed in sweat, twists with full attention:
The hilly snaking is an effort; you wonder who's in pain.

The load-like people breathe fearfully as they gasp solemnly;
Prayerfully, not to god but to the cracking pieces' December.
Like a flecking 17th century building, the lorry's pieced up, dressed under
To keep it day-by-day and it survives through any thunder.
Day and night it snakes, twists it way up; the load praying randomly.

The hill conquered, the rumble, roar, dies down, the fear phase passed.
Then the load's souls sneak back stealthily, entering each owner
As the smile on the soot-faced, blood-eyed, yolk-colored teethed
Driver's face lit his way up the mocking and unmerciful hill under
Whose trees sheltered undergrowth laugh at the driver who *hissed*.

Because they are all in pain, with southern sounds

Diamond Seeded Mango's Cage

Where her hidden pearls grabbed a nap, taking
A siesta like an unprovoked jungle lion,
A naive ingrate, maybe!

Where dry desert, chill earth creations, find meaning
In a diamond headed populace that defies push and
Relegation into the abyss, an unmerciful
Depth of hellish discomfort, *medievals* they are perhaps!

Where civilization laboured, bore every bit of shiny
Hope crystal, colored by golden grips of nature's
Purity, grip then so hard, yet never lasted; she remains
Empty emptiness, lazy hand, but how now?

Where she thought she had it all: might, riches
Beauty, nature's consent, pride, she's now addled,
Crumpled in distemper, she holds no value,
Makes no value, seen as no value, she spreads her seeds
Everywhere, now she folds her
Arms and says:
'At least I'm a mango with A diamond seed.'

As I Die Slowly

Eating through
Undeterred
Cognizant
Of the world left to him
To rummage
To his full fill
Not worried
Though because
His meals
Are left him
For e-*finishing.*

Dragon Unleashed (1)

Clad by that tattered purple pullover, she stared at me
On the river bank with black and white sincerity and
delight.
But why did she pick it up?
Oh, 'cause it looked glassy?
Yes, it looked gelatinous like toad eggs
Slowly and heavenly swaying on a pool of priestly waters.
That kid innocently played with the venomous snake
Lurking under those pretentiously heavenly waters.
That colorless, invisible snake laid its insolent pangs
On those precious innocence, the kids.
They're left there…beckoned and owned by poverty, tossed
Into pauperism as no one shoulders the blame.
Naïve and sincere Samaritans squeeze their purses
Out only for the gravity to mock them dry.
Now the insolent snake has the chance because of the
failures of the concerned.
He preys on the kids. Now, these kids see
Every shiny article on the water and run to it,
And see every gelatinous deliciousness and lick it.
They have no civilized conscience or knowledge to care
And be self-aware.
They're perhaps innocent of perils under those gentle
ripples,
Maybe they'd owned pauperism for being disowned:
The epic disowned by blood and now disowned
By principles.
The monster finishes her in my watch so fast!
Whose fault? The society is shirking, disavowing.

Dragon Unleashed (2)

Tom said it couldn't get him.
He was cleaned and preserved:
Nature valued.
I didn't know he was wrong,
Like a *fatwa* patient he
Assumed impeccable policing
In favor because of his nature.

But now, sprawled in bed, his body
Sucked to the bone, his eyes
Buried in his socket, he looked
Like a scary movie character.
I was the vulnerable one then,
But now he calls and whispers,
Slowly
And gently like
Summer wind through baby plant leaves:

"It's everyone's,
It takes no bribes, eats all kinds
Of food; it's poor; it's rich:
Just about everyone."

Only a Jungle Beast, They Say.

She has spread her demonic
Wings over that island, and
Chiselled her lengthy canine
To push it through the island's heart
Down to the bottom of the ocean,
Helpless, weak-kneed, the island
Stares in awe, dragon unleashed
Upon it, but the *unleashists*
Assume innocence, the island
Demands why only her,
'How many islands nature built?'
But the dragon, the
Demonic apparition knows no tongue,
 Unleashists says,
It doesn't spare her either,
But the dragon's pangs are not too deep
Inside the *unleashists*' own
Unlike the focused island.
The *Focused Island* is silenced, gagged
But believed culpable.

Midday Dust Storm

I'd slept through the midday heat like
A drugged mental patient, then I'd woken
Up like a scared chicken.

I lazily looked out of the window and dragged
My unwilling feet out, taken aback by the howl,
Not mistaking the storm's sprawl.

As always the order, everything snagged,
Flying, dust-conquered, and then I sat bitten,
My eyes sand-filled, scotching sun at 40s, bitin'

With sand blindness, body sweating, I shrugged
Off the dust that was sweat-diluted: that was the livin'!
Burnt by red-hot sun, dehydrated, I sat on a 'divan'.

To Disport Myself When the Pylon IS Cut

For late John Garang ë Mabior, PhD

Joy is costly but, to them, sorrow is incredibly cheap,
Disparaging milestones are disparate to rip;
The pylon's gone, the incredible journey's stanchion

No one will call a spade; they're seen as glades,
Because continuity is throttled, when blades,
After the war and plight, are abandoned.

Abandonment questioned! Care questioned!
They need grits and strength to brace his stationed
Sumptuous standpoint to close the gate of neo-thraldom.

They'll row the Nile, snow-teethed, their sorrow concealed.
He needed not cries, no threnody either, but hands cleaned
To pride on the davenports and finish Nile's length in
stardom.

Exegesis of Despotism

Their peak of denial appeals, creeps
Into havens of only hypo's[4] when the just keeps
Justice inbuilt, covered and unused, sinners toot
Away purportedly, the vehement veil of the wicked booth,
And then dance projecting goodness in broad daylight;
Goodness that collapses like flimsy sheet of soap foam, comes night,
But who bathes clean the concealment? Wickedness buried just for show,
And the just covers goodness for survival, crystal dichotomy though
Hidden and timed for bad and good, despotic podium's always high,
And seen will it not be service for the trodden who'll never sigh
And say, perhaps 'nature needs us here. Lucky us', but fortune
Of the destitute naps too long for enough, and fortune
Of the despot stays bright and shine, for it eats big and plant ample petard
That the weak squirm with their words only squeezed out in fright, hard
And desired, and the master joyous, drifting, sailing high in ecstasy
Far beyond the leaps and hops of his iron hands, 'cause his scratchy
Demeanour's bitter, but surprised will we always be
As he draws riches, fame and strength, we see
His friends, mighty and 'moral', from far nations, from his circle,
The keepers of order, he says it, the weak prostrate like oracle
Has breathed damnation over an ancient hamlet, but again,
Confused will we always be as the wicked sees every gain
And lobbies support to his den, full and a fool, yet
The weak by trial and supplication are always at their set.

---

[4] Exceptionally callous hypocrites

Montreal Summer Sunset

You couldn't get up, spread
On the river bank as the darkness
Crawled slowly toward the light and the orange
Arctic sun dived down behind St. Lawrence.

The breeze and the soothing feel out
Of the river, cemented you onto the
Pavement by the river and you watched
The sun's orange tongue as it tasted
The edge of the horizon, there, nothing
 Else you could call for.

As the sun enjoyed the sweetness
Of the horizon's sugary powder, it
Increased its tongue's size deep
Into the horizontal bottom to enjoy
Its meal, but you wished a rope around it,

The strongest of all ropes around the sun
To pull it up, but the darkness swallowed
You slowly, then you peered back and saw
The city lit up, so you limped back
To the city's rowdiness; having broken
The glue that'd then fixed you down…
And your failure to fix the sun.

The Avaricious Owl

The wise, the learned and the
Slicker, polish and spread
Their canvass prolix to quench
The insatiable avarice of the wise.
When the cannonade echoes
Melt down, the canopy of
Praised impotent pool
Of edited farrago sank…
could there be sumptuous fascia?

The Nilotic Beam

The elephant trunk curved and whitened;
Placed neatly and befittingly above your
Arm's crook, strangled your bicep and blended
With the sizzling milk, the foam atop the jug
As you pulled the udder with passion and skill,
Your thick bosom and responsible thighs
Securely sandwiched the jug with a firm grip.

Your fingers swiftly pressing like hands on fire,
Your palms as dark as a charcoal placed
On a snowy ground, you finished milking
With a laughing felicity,
And you sat by the fire cooking your mum's meal.

But you boiled me happy with those tiny, evenly
Trimmed teeth that nature planted on that black gum,
The night stealthily comes and I clandestinely lay
By you surrounded by mooing cattle heads
We mindlessly stare at the cloudless sky as
The moonlight scattered the tiny grains of stars;
Evenly spread on the sheet of that bluish canvass.

Hope Candelabrum

Impasse ahead, drilled potholes, but they still muse
With hearts lined with hope candelabrum,
Though the declivity is freshly debugged.

The humility debtor appreciates the use
Though the Decalogue is not decathlon hum
And we all appreciate the huff roan subbed.

Sarah's milieu still braced me to deduce
That, with stilt, charm of past narks, that my bum
Wasn't a choice, your dekkos, hands, cuffed…

Cinnamon Haunted

In the mellow cogency to hex demoniacal,
Drinking cognac with lilac and jocose tentacle,
The mind, hand, the regent debacle after the hiatus
Have always pushed the stars off my sky, the status
Of denial when the morning dew; the obstacle
That has had you off-shore, scared at grass's call.
Now heaven knows it hadn't poised for buffalo's puss,
The cinnamon faces under the jacaranda, the bus
Filled with pallid masters that now skip the obstacle,
Don't even look the captions as ethos neat the fingerstall
Even the nightingale, the eagle and the crow, discuss
In their own natural echoes, we can now take no fuss
With our Decalogue, the chosen will smile with the ball
In their court, but who will detach the string, and install
The love podium, well sorry! All stand above
With no one under the platform, so good to have
The unctuous guess, but is everyone served?

SECTION FOUR

Religion, Nature, Being and Perceptions

Poetic Preamble 4

Religion has both the admired elements of *beauty,* and its dreadful *monstrosity* in historical time. Historically informed cosmopolitans would remember that the Vatican has persecuted many people in the name of *god.* All the Papal Inquisitions were meant to protect the church.[5] Religion was also used in some cases to support slavery and suppress causes that were meant to bring some social equality or equity to human beings of all *races* and works of life. Bertrand Russell, in *Why I am Not a Christian*, writes that

> The churches, as everyone knows, opposed the abolition of slavery as long as they dared, and with a few well-advertised exceptions they opposed at the present day every movement towards economic justice. The pope has officially condemned Socialism.[6]

However, the poems in this section are not meant to lament the *Inquisitions* or the negative effects religion has meted out on Africans and other "Co-Third-Worlders", "*unfortunates.*" What's presented in this section is the intellectual aspect of religion and how it relates to existential acceptance of all human beings in the 21st century. *Pious Rascals* and *Against Jejune Fidelity* challenge the inherent assumption—the

---

[5] See Bertrand Russell's *Why I am Not a Christian*, (edited by Paul Edwards) New York, Touchstone Books, 1957, p.20.
[6] Russell, *Why I am Not a Christian*, p.26.

infallibility of religious dogmatisms—that makes religious leaders and their assumptions dangerous to the average theist, the sceptical theist and the atheist.

While the humane and beneficial side of religion—the proven hope-engendering humanitarianism—is a necessary social element in our society, there's another side of religion that's pretentiously dangerous and divisive.

True Piety explains exactly the reason why religion is an indispensable part of our contemporary society. It explains how Catholic nuns give their lives to help poor African children get education for the betterment of their [African] lives. This poet is a beneficiary of such 'True Piety.'

What About Answers? makes us speculatively wonder about the nature of some of the things we take for granted throughout our daily lives. '*What about Blackness?*' asks pertinent questions about the *truth* of religion and the inter-racial derivatives that make religion seem racially *owned*.

Were it not my inability
Would there be god?
....
Were it not for your nature's inadequacies
Would you hate me?
...
Were it not for disdain
Would there be terror?
...

Essentially, inter-racial, inter-class perceptions, judgements, and prejudgements, are captured in *The 'they' Conundrum*, *Scalpels of the Throng*, *The Hair* and *Confidence*.

So let's reflect with clean consciences and worship with informed piety.

What About Blackness?

She mocked eventualities and eternal nonexistence;
Everyday she waited for absenteeism of emergence...
Emergence of self-righteous men, *the chosen*.
They were lords of the east who adorned the ozone,
Her perspicuous nobleness smells personalities.
The magenta top spoke of grits to indignities...
We've always assumed her base niche with ease
As her fingers itched with chilliness of winter tease.
The bulbous, chalky sand dunes by the road
Had the hairy, pallid lad smile despite being wrought.
I've always smiled with light-heartedness to blend in,
Poor us! She'd written books of the *born-chosen* din.
Wondered all the dorks of all geographies!
The chosen weren't coming back, *never*: philosophies!
Pure philosophies had her tower, her eyes hidden;
Hidden by the dark complexion: we stared, ridden!
But she questioned the *exceptionalism* of the heavens,
The nobleness of the chose, and their ever-smiling servants.
The mockers smiled with preponderance of *schmuckness*...
Lord, she smiled and amply said: *What about blackness!!*

Pious Rascals

I've seen the *transcendental writs* of Russell,
They've laid waste morality of *a* rascal;
Who'd professed the providence's dogmatism,
It was the medieval misuse of truism.
There's no such a thing gauged by the providence;
Providence's idealism is a coinage of the power essence,
Which had thrust a sizeable number into prominence,
I doubt if truth's quiddity wouldn't be in silence,
Insecurities of the *cherished flaws* prevail,
They've been tried but they still prevail,
Riches and propaganda are the order,
The pious rascals wear shame disorder,
That's why they never notice its disastrous effect;
Perhaps livelihood makes them assume to disinfect
The real moralists, suffering as truth martyrs,
The *cherished flaws* still, to the pious, matters,
The pious moralists feast with *blood* and *gusto*
But the hanged moralists will exist also.

The Cosmological Balls

I know that big ball
Matters all that much,

The relative small
One does so as such,

But the *cosmic*
Frowns at the absolute,

Calls it relative ontic:
I claim the opposite
Just like a brute,

A dot on the small
 Ball (I) is at rest,
 Short of absolute,

Don't mind,
Discount the big ball
And bless the absolute,

I'll sacrifice myself
And mock the
Moustached fellow,

I rest absolutely on the
Small ball, my small world:
The *housing environment*.

I'll Wipe Them and Say Your Name Loud

I don't know the crux of my Kantian space,
But I know I'm waiting, a dire supplication,
A meridian solace, but I'm waiting. When you
Saw that tall man peering down on me under
That infertile, black coconut tree, you'd told me:
'Be humble son…he did cross your path,
But you crossed his too,'…I'd spelled my…
My wonder! I did cross his path,
But I'm waiting, still waiting. I still
Say my name loud, but look around for you.

I'm still waiting but for what, Hume will tell me.
I'd gone to church but the pallid brothers showed,
Told me I burned down my hut and came to theirs.
You'd warned me against the arctic brothers' ways.
"Come for the right way, come to the light" they'd said.
Platonic allegory appealed to me…
Now going to church is a tall man's pace,
I'm too short and you know that…I just miss
What you told me…"say your name loud!"

I'm still waiting, perhaps you're waiting too.
But you'd tutored me enough not to complain.
The world is a neat sadness as you'd said,
But I want you to stand in that snowy garment they
Always told me you wear now… and say out loud,
That I'd not gone astray. That confused man
Upstairs perhaps wasn't sure of his job description
When he lied about *free will*, can you tell him
He's malevolent like some eastern brothers?

I'm not complaining, I just don't like the man
Upstairs, and I don't know what to make of the
Throng downstairs, but I do know behind that
Impressive unimaginable, you smile magnificently
And yell: "Say your name loud!"
With those words, I'll wipe them off now, and
Say *my* name loud.

Against Jejune Fidelity

Whether damned,
Spooked, spurned,
Stripped of significance;
Image caricatured by all,
At least, not to mention
The providence treasure
That's weighed to serve her
The least and draw her the weak.
But the iron heart builds
The fancy of her might
Like a lioness tamed to harm
No tourists, and there
Has her nature enjoyed
When stripped of pride—strength.

Her existence with
Equity, to be seen and see
That which strikes naivety,
Breeds the essence
Of her cosmic indispensability
With paradox when she inks
To convey the hardest she does—thought!

She's the truest path that withers the
Mired hate and thought extermination,
When touching the untouchable,
And pen—speak the unspeakable,
To stamp the soul of *needability*,
Of that dark voice, to lay crap
The tired dogmas and expose vapid piety.

Now they want to see her down,
But she will speak and exist not exit!

A Ghostly Paragon

(*For the African Mother*)

She procures a debilitating
Peek, though short-lived, it
Pierces through 'arrogant' hearts
Like amber laser beams
Guarding a room fixed of
Valuables and full of the same.

She gathers her self
Adeptly; full of zeal,
Truest imagination,
Like she existed before
Everyone else did,
A nonpareil being she might
Think.

But dubious shall I remain.
Cynical might I be!
I sneeze out my wonder,
Or better still, say: jealousy.

She holds up the star, with it
I'm seen; pushes off meteorites
When they dare fall on me;
Guard me from flood when
It's up to ruin my harvest and me.

She's nothing but the spirit
Of the dreadful black cat that I at times
Ridicule; the ghostly fix with

Unimaginable protectiveness,
Holds me head high.

Spite Allayer I (Turning the Other Cheek)

Like a comatose lizard
I will slumber with my distinct and
Spotless instincts marred, dismissed
Like a medieval eidolon.
Even if scotched, crumpled,
Twisted by fixed realities,
I will oftentimes with teeth
Showing, like a chortle
Machine, supplant crude
Cattiness into muse and
Scream out: *I love you the more
You hit.*

The Chameleon Mercies

In red, clad in
Feigned glory:
Their strengths, but
Even in that cubicle
They were

Societal risks
And grace
By law and disdain…
Not their own though.

Their conscience
Fluffed, derogated,
They knew not the
Quiddity of their being.

But the box and bars like them;
Perhaps they're needed
To ascribe to ancestral
Orthodoxy: docility.
.

Feeler for Roses

Between Scylla
And Charybdis, her
Soul will always…
Not slumber, no.

The ghosts of cosmos
And seraphic deceits
Will always trample
On her, like 'witches'
In the middle time.

Her nutritious-ness is
Indispensable, but she's still
Wished into Auschwitz.

She doesn't inhale why
She's thought down.
She only wished they
Knew her!

The Bus Driver

He struggled with the
Steering wheel. Even though
His navy blue uniform
fitted him good, his cap
Bestowing honour, he squirms
Uncomfortably on his seat.

He wore a face of horror,
Breathing anger like a hellish
Welding beam flame, I guess
A bad night he might have had:
The wife perhaps, a girl
Friend maybe, but what
Had I in there… for he sent
Me the door?

Spite Allayer II (Altruism)

Build no house
But build a strong
Will…in the heart.

Inspire acrid verbose
lexicon,
But expire rosier says
To the tirade stringed
To you: and pray

For pestilence, hydra,
Will come not your
Way, your foes will
Go prostrate for you…
'Cause you're enduring,

Innocence in honesty:
With it you canonize
Togetherness!
Believe them not…
Remarkable you'll look.

Even the Numb Nature Needs Joy

Plants will always be planted and harvested;
Animals will bear, be admired, eaten and vested
With undesired remains, but rested
Might everything seem even when tested.

Denial courts people, but still the rain rains,
Crops sprout, grass grows, animals' grazing stains:
Assumption. They bear healthy kids: 'free' gains;
Free even when hurtled tough soil, no brains.

Now, they'll march to their shade, rough but singing
And ringing bells tied on their necks; clinging
For joy, tattoos now for pride, then comes the blinking;
Blinking painfully for few drops of rain, enjoying.

True Piety

For the JRS sisters

In that aridness she preferred to melt with us,
To her homeland shade she didn't want to go,
In us she'd found children to nurture, her purpose.

She perched her aging hat low over her eyes,
Planted her glasses nose-tip-length away,
Though tired and darkened by heat and dust,
She didn't want to go to her cool homeland
Education must 'these poor souls get!'
For in our success lay her joy.

We didn't come from her kind womb in essence,
Difference was considerable, color a wicked testimonial,
But difference it didn't make for with her we had a mother,
Day and night she saw us go,
Day and night she toiled for us,
Who knew if she even slept a single day to rest…?
But now she can sleep and rest for she wasn't wrong…
Not to sleep.

What about Answers?

Were it not for the living,
 Would there be a ghost?

Were it not for the sin,
Would there be righteousness?

Were it not my inability,
Would there be gods?

Were it not for the sordid,
Would there be belle?

Were it not for Samaritans,
Would there be paupers?

Were it not for the East,
Would we have West?

If we all laughed,
Who'd cry?

If we all lived,
Who then died?

Self confidence in all,
But how about subservience?

Were it not for the congregation,
Would there be a priest?

Were it not for disorder,

Would there be Presidents?

Were it not for information,
Would there be *The Press*?

Were it not for your nature's inadequacies,
Would you hate me?

Were it not for the mouth,
Would down there be open?

If god protected us,
Who'd then crave doctors?

If life is a pack of endurance,
Why then live to suffer?

Were it not for disdain,
Would there be terror?

But because of the rich,
We have the poor!

If you didn't fear me,
Would you hate me?

If I was weakness all through,
Would you worry about me?

If I can't do it to your desire,
Would you shut me out?

Let me try perhaps,

Nature will judge me off!

Do you reject me vehemently
Because you think I'd take over?

Sure! I mean something!
That's why you fear me, not that
You're great, see future, not history.

If you made it, it'll come back
For you and sing: *thank you*!

Word Document!

As I sat down, my rear-bottom itched
And my body snake-twisted I writhed:
Freeze-wristed the keys defied my push,
Mocking with no letter, ooh! (Pain) I hush!

Your squared front stared at me, rude,
As if I'd cynically lied about my frozen joints
That stupefied me; still you think I could?
The weather feels me not: you got the points?

But you still remained blank with no thanks,
As if I'm not to grace you beautiful with words,
That'd make me glad, you hip like lush river banks,
No felled trees, revealing grace…not just woods.

Scalpels of the Throng

Miles out of my mind, I will stand and meditate
About me and the floweret that's been trimmed,
Though I'm not a threat, no one will strap sanity
Around me, not that anyone did before, but the glittering
Scalpels angled by the fiery throng, taking me for
A trajectory of treacherous tommyrot, will never
 Scratch me at least.

My tomfoolery and shabby insolence will make me
Defy the essence of arctic and oriental ontologies, the stars,
The cross and the curvy moon always laughing at my
Joy, a sorrow for them to jump when I'm briskly
Walking. Will I also defy the heavenly cross?
The weak sun, sun of all might, grip, grit and greed!
I have a hand, if not a mouth and a mind.

Finding Cracks in Walls

I

In the church they were many
And he never wanted to choose any

By the mosque, he saw self-righteousness,
Confidence, and rigidity, but he was fluidness
And suppleness.

In the temple he meditated with conspicuousness,
Trying enlightenment, he slept with mad seriousness.

In the synagogue he tried to blend in, but there he was,
Who did he think would care? Guess would a horse!

'I'll love, spread togetherness, not finding cracks
In every religious and social walls,' he learnt.

II

In search of his high school heart, he failed.
She's dead, he feared, but no, she was a praised
Feminist and MARRIED.

He bumped into her just a month
Into his search: 'You look familiar,' he muttered

'Deng, I remember you, why not me, too?'
'So changed you are, so lost you are, and now
Getting you is a blessing,' he rapped,

"When did your mum divorce your dad?"
He inquired.
'God forbid!' she exclaimed.

'Like a pauper who'd lost his only dollar, I've
Searched, asked, googled you, and nothing
Was there,' he'd said.

He realized *people* disappear with marriage!
It was a surprise not a crack on the wall this time.
He mused and adjusted his smiling hat.

III

Fatima's hijab always on, bright and as beautiful
As eagle's head. She silently muttered the day's last prayer,

She'd hoped to sit in front, and tell them the *Allah* she loves
More than anything, she could cry his name loud, but no!

Her Christian friend had told her, that her mum, like
A chicken out of the shelter into the rain, had run
Out of the church for her dear life:
She'd praised priesthood, feminine priesthood.

Fatima had hoped to bring temple into the mosque, but
A scalpel ten inches from her jaws, she was numbed,

'Let's take the given and stop finding cracks,'
Her would-have-been-her-man, had told her.

Contentment I

The garage's dingy
And muddled, but
He still praises
The rusting
Testimony;
A gonzo species I'd say.

Contentment II (Stygian)

By my eye I'll cry by my sty,
    The cleaned line creamed and I sigh

By my eyes, my hearing has become full,
    Enough filtered in: bad and good. I'm still cool?

By my body, by my skin, blown the mocking breeze,
    The blanched look, spotless, but stygian increase.

By my hair stood defiance, shampoo mocked, laughed at,
    Because, unkempt, shaggy and I shabby, shall we add?

The 'They' Conundrum

They never listened
They never talked to us
They never believed us

They never worked for us
They worked to eat
They lied and stole

They persecuted us for our deeds
They raped our kids
Our mums, our sisters' pride,
Our hope, our life

They resisted order
They were served the order
They never appreciated the order

They knew nothing
They believed nothing
They achieved nothing

They ate everything
They drank everything
They had nothing

They gave the punch
They came to stop us
They went away scot-free

They are slick
They can every time sneak

And they can change quick

They show you the skin
They show the teeth clean
But they lean and sing hate glimpse

They blame history
They never wrote history
History is people made

They can kiss the freedom
They cried for freedom
They abused the freedom

They have a weak heritage
They agree with us
They have history to help us

They have been shown the way
They are weak to follow the way
They are fast to blame us anyway

When will they stop to whine?
And when will they climb
The ladder of the world trend? With time?

They have no one to blame
They have themselves to praise
Yet they have us to blame

We brought them the pride
They still trample the drive
And they misuse the trials

They evolved with time
Forty years is faster an evolution time
Yet we are not the Divine

They took the time
They had not any hearts
They killed for pleasure

They were the civilized
They had us Christianized
They still think we are uncivilized

They bred terror, civilized and archaic
They now blame jejune impiety
They are to blame, they are the uncivilized

Rustic Ordeals

The novel napalm is colourfully testimonial,
Bigger is the archaic upsurge of denial.
What about locusts' meals on trees?
The cactus glades and sheets of sudd reeds?

The tired rustics gather their saddlebags
And scuttle like lobsters jesting around snags,
The chameleons deserve appreciation.
Can forgiveness be forged for feigned faction?

When the long johns are given with praise debt,
Even the lion's imperialism would flourish the best
To the tinkling twist of nuts outer sequin
That hoists the septic bastion unlike the plasticine.

Synod Aspirations

If I see wizened edelweiss in the tropics,
Snow and grizzled snow bears
In the dessert, you will as well
Grin as it might be
My dementia or wishful dreams.

If Jupiter was my éclat, echelon topics
There are, and I eddy, or hop,
Snares will not leave me.
You might as well chill,
The red planet and stars all
Remember the dark's screams.

I ran helter skelter,
Lived the same: the optics,
The surgicals, mechanics, drives,
Sails; all the shares of buffaloes' sizzle—
Whining but still the synod's
Secrets embosomed the sulked teams.

The Winter

The folks, the land and the weather,
Take their wishes as the snow plans
 A come back with that sheet
Of alabaster sand to flood us,

The blanched environs and the
Spread snow's blanket evince
The purity unblemished, though
Annoyingly pressing in the chill bites,

The whiteness, epical of
The bridle land, the white snow
Spread everywhere, the bloodless
House blending with snowy
Architecture and the pallid
Kid standing at the window:
'I like it here dad,' he said.

When Pigs Lend Hands

Would you praise the farrows
If they salvage your coffers?
Crass and bathed in conspicuous acridness,
I might as well guess your sanguinary
To sashay you above the rim of greed.
You might as well feign *deistic*
Might, or grin, laugh: a satyr.
You might be none the human
You are, but the parvenu will live to
Eat, thank gods living is a season and the
Satyr might as well vanish; the ghost
A figment of mere imagination.

Your hair

The straightened fur didn't speak to me,
But the other rolls I've come to see:
Disorderly, dropping *rastafarispeak*,
Like a fixed post you said your creek.

Confidence

Why is confidence supposed a word to everyone
When all can't shoot a glimpse at it even once?

Joel rode in a mighty cloud praising his dad,
But when he missed his grip he blamed the cat.

Wondered the dunker-skull? He tore his pants
And like an amateur skater slipped: mere cants?

Well, the cat's blame had him fall on a rat;
We'd wonder if the cat blamed it on the rest.

'Gee! Dad it wasn't easy,' Joel cried
Again, 'spread your leg,' he was tried

'I know it's not genetic to skate, but rate
Your family to fly; fly above a just glade.

SECTION FIVE

Appreciation

Poetic Preamble 5

Family is the most important phenomenon nature has given us besides positive feeling about oneself. This section is a celebration of life and family. Our family members value us in our lows and highs. When I lost my father in 2003, everything, for me, went downhill. Nothing I saw made any sense, not even education. I still haven't recovered from his loss, but the thought that he'd brought up a person like me gives me strength to write everyday.

I found consolation in writing poetry, nonfiction and fiction. He's the biggest and the greatest reason of why I write. *Just the Other Day* is my celebration of the second year anniversary of my daughter's birth. *Strength of Your Whisper* is my reflection on my relationship with my family.

Festive City is a celebration of Montreal's vibrancy; a city that has so much to offer in terms of intellectualism, tourism and culture. It's in Montreal that I came to understand a larger part of the person I am now. The consolidation of my thoughts brought about by both the loss of my father and the serenity of my life in Montreal awakened me to the reality of me being a *writer*.

Everything became clear as the clouds covering 'Who am I?' started to clear. I became fully aware of myself and my place in the world; what Martin Heidegger would call my *presence-in-the-world* my *dasien*, or understanding of my *sense of self* as both an *object* and a *subject* in the world in a Fanonian sense.

However, there's no *sense of self* without the thought that you have a loving family you can count on, in whatever way. The mere fact that I had and have a loving family kept me living and writing.

And in Montreal I learnt to appreciate the simple things in life which I could have back home[7], termed silly. I learnt to say 'Thank You' every now and then. I also came to realize that my father raised a man who appreciated everything but didn't know how to *ground* this sense in *a* self as an *object to be rationalized* and *judged,* and also as a *subject* to *interpret* the world and *judge* others. I started to appreciate what I have: family, my engendered environment, and above all, my *talents*. I also learnt that being Racist is not necessarily a question of hate or ignorance; it could also be a question of fear and uncertainty as to how one should approach racial issues against others as both *objects* and *subjects.*

Understanding oneself is therefore paramount. A not-so-worthy African-American clergy, David James Manning of ATLAH ministries[8], once argued that 'black' people can be trained to be anything: doctors, astronauts, lawyers, engineers, but, he argued, they don't understand the world. However, understanding the world starts with a clear understanding of *one self.* Without understanding of *oneself,* understanding the world becomes a gigantic, mocking monstrosity. David Manning has no any idea about who he

---

[7] South Sudan
[8] Just google his name to see the nature of the man he is and what his social, political and religious teachings are.

is. The world he thinks he understands is inspired by a small, tenth square mile of Harlem and his proselytization behind bars. A man who understands himself takes bitterness with smiles and humility, yet still, confronts all the things he dislikes with combative civility.[9] That, I appreciate!

---

[9] See 1987 *Cry Freedom* movie about Steve Bantu Biko (Trial Scene)

Just the Other Day

On the plane I knew you'd sweeten my life,
As I touched down you made me sigh;
Enthusiasm the word, you blessed my world.
You gave me among other things a word:
Just the other day I became a Father!

Just the other day you made me smile
After all these years of dreadful time,
Daddy left and I was empty emptiness,
Believe me; you've brought me sweetness,
Just the other day you made me a Father.

I'd lost my smile when his news came,
I'd lost my smile when calls became the same,
I'd lost my heart when my words annoyed,
It was all for the good of us I employed,
But you came bubbling over with energy.

You sweetly brought my smile back,
I see your beautiful face when I reflect,
It seems just like the other day indeed,
But hey, happy, happy birthday Atetdit.
A thousand candles await.

Festive City

Festivity suffused, delight
Filled, the mother of laughs
Pours her romping romance
With her wings spread
In harness, like a
Pacifist strong hold:
Singing, musing
For delight at
St. Lawrence view
Of the diving, orange sun,
Old port edging
Like she's taking a
Sip of the river's water,
Mt. Royal raises
Her neck, a pylon
Of delight seekers.
When the night stealthily
Pushes light away, the
Fun seekers, drunk with
Fun, of material and
Sentimentality, walk with friends
And dovetail their fingers;
Strolling in the breeze of St. Catherine
Street, McGill College Avenue winks
In anticipation, McGill licks her lips
In welcome, McCord cries that
She has it all if passed by.
The day ends with hardly
Enjoyment at ten sights,
What'd it be like tomorrow?

The Strength of Your Whisper

When you whispered your whisper
Sang to me loud, gracing, chancing me;
The words that dwarf all wisdoms, claiming
Might so powerful so touching …
But why did you go?

The deeds are for *self* but deeper,
Like the depth of unmerciful oceans, seas
That have been feasting on me, *claiming*
The ones who lived, epical of all doings:
Dad why did you go?

I live by your words: my true keeper,
Words that steer me through all just to see,
The world that I spurn is my making,
As we see it as true hypocrites,
But your going makes the world big.

I can't row alone, dad! Why did you go?

When Nature is Questioned

He bequeathed what he cherished, the only thing he had,
His natures probity at best, the only thing that
Mattered to him: sharing.

He never had a silver spoon, but he was a golden giver;
Planted with a golden heart to grace his immediate
Hardship with the dreams he shared.

Nature's ways are never known, but he was
Seen gradually and gracefully vanishing;
Just like all powerful goodie powers, ceding
Everything to a new evil heart that gnawed with
No remorse.

Mum

She's always said, there
Is the world, here is the word,
Remember him, your dad, the perfect
Man there was: short, joyous,
Resourceful and caring.
Will you evince the same?
She'd asked me, but less slicker
Have I always seen myself:
Weak-kneed, peppery-mouthed,
But the canned hope she presented
Me guarded and consoled me when she was
Near, and now thousands of miles
Away, her advice's a solace;
Opening my soul's mouth
Wide and receiving,
Like a thirst patient:
Mouth opened, tongue extended
Out long and dry in a searing,
Scotching heat of the desert sand.
Nothing keeps me here, but her will.

Blessings of Bridge Builders

(To all Calgary Bridge Foundation for Youth Workers)

Welcome to Calgary, Alberta, Canada!

The plane hovered around with shady figures below us;
Touching down, the window allowed us a rare glimpse.
By the window, an unfamiliar whiteness covered things like cars,
The morning arrived and stinging sensations tested our dreams.
The insufferable chill bit our feet, fingers and ears.

Our new, confusing home!

On the streets everything looks the same when John asks.
'Where is hope of dream fulfilment?'...if hope gleams!
The bus sailed smoothly as we followed the crowds.
"This is the end," the driver smiled to our innocent chagrin.
We were lost in a sea of strangeness to our greatest fears.

Being lost and being helped!

After hours of city wide ride we arrived, bus after bus.
Strangers in a strange land were late and ashamed to their brims,
But the lady behind a huge yellow desk smiled amply with stars:
"Welcome to Kingsland!" Our late, lowered faces smiled to disbeliefs:
Late but understood, scared but with someone who endears.

The welcoming heart!

The smiling lady was a consoling stop we took for a Canadian buss,
Another smiling face, a man, brought back our steams.
The 'Welcome to Canada' sign at the airport echoed as kindness starts;
The web of complexity and cloud of uncertainty opened way to teem;
To teem us with 'you're in safe hands,' that I thought of giving her beers.

Getting meaningful help!

We smiled our way home knowing we were off the morning ruckus,
Two weeks later and our coffers were quickly deflating, it seems…
Kids were bored afterschool; John's job-search creating mental scars.
Then an endearing phone call brought back our Canadian esteems.
Remember the smiling lady? she sent souls who were good ears.

Getting settled by the smiling minds!

The library became our playing field: swimming, reading and browsing,
My children's boredom died the day of the endearing voice's calling,
John's loneliness frowned away with a book club, workshops and training,
John Jr. had friendly-faced mentors and he competes for good mannerism.
A good ear, a good word, a humble heart… checks for John and I.

Thanks and blessing for the smiling face, the first bridge builder!

And for us I thank the smiling face, the first bridge builder,
After school children see smiling hearts with lovely programs,
In school and after school we count on smiling minds for guidance,
And for better jobs we now know how to meaningfully say: 'gimme a job'.
Blessed be the bridge builders; the smiling face connected us.

**** Thök de ka ***

Kuir ë Garang is a South Sudanese poet, writer and author currently living in Calgary, Alberta. For more information about the author and all his writings, visit his website at
www.kuirthiy.com

www.ingramcontent.com/pod-product-compliance
Lightning Source LLC
Chambersburg PA
CBHW070454100426
42743CB00010B/1613